Fire or Fire

# Fire or Fire

*Poems*

Rosanne Coggeshall

Louisiana State University Press

*Baton Rouge*

MM

Copyright © 1987, 1991, 1999, 2000 by Rosanne Coggeshall
Manufactured in the United States of America
First printing
09  08  07  06  05  04  03  02  01  00
5  4  3  2  1

Designer: Melanie O'Quinn Samaha
Typeface: Sabon
Printer and binder: Thomson-Shore, Inc.

Library of Congress Cataloging-in-Publication Data:

Coggeshall, Rosanne, 1946–
    Fire or fire : poems / Roseanne Coggeshall.
      p. cm.
    ISBN 0-8071-2627-6 (alk. paper)—ISBN 0-8071-2628-4 (pbk. : alk. paper)
      I. Title

    PS3553.O4155 F57 2000
    811'.54—dc21                                              00-034530

The author gratefully acknowledges the editors of the following publications, in
which some of the poems herein first appeared, some in slightly different form:
*The Hollins Critic:* "Kalanchoe"; *Shenandoah:* "Weatherman," "Another
Round"; *South Carolina Review:* "Prayer for the Whole State," "For All the
Saints"; *Southern Review:* "Motions of the Heart," "Walking Pawleys Island."

Many thanks to Laura Oaks for her help.

In memory of my mother and grandmothers
For my father and Peter, Amelia, and Peg

Who then devised the torment? Love.
Love is the familiar Name
Behind the hands that wove
The intolerable shirt of flame
Which human power cannot remove.
    We only live, only suspire
    Consumed by either fire or fire.
        —T. S. Eliot, "Little Gidding"

# Contents

### III

Augustine Said

### IV

Rivets (New Poems)

# I

## Cyclic

# Warriors

We have all dreamed of moons,
of waters parting,
of armies punishing, up
through rushes on the other side—

blue moons, half moons,
moons like cuticles
in stars sheerer
than dust.

Always
there are circles,
infinities of light, sutured, with no end—
and the sole night weapon:
a wickless fire,
carved from nothing,
fed neither by branches
nor by drifts
of fossil fuel.

Armies stagger, vanish.
Waters close: *Applause.*
Above, the solitary sun singles out
each filament of flesh and rinses it
in fused rhapsodies of light.

# L.A. Artist

The fires, you say, have disappeared.
Charred wood & rubble intersect;
blackened concrete & asphalt,
spurred with shattered glass,
glisten through headlights when patrol cars pass.
The street is quiet now.

On his bike,
an adolescent sways
from left to right,
across spiked pavement.

Apart, light in your room
like permission,
you exercise your present—
this as random
as the moon's carved curve,
caught in night's charry glance.

## To J. O. Hurt, M.D.

I come into your hospital
like a ragman, holding splinters,
scattering thorns and nails.
There is something in my mind
that fails to further,
fails to furnish corridors with light.
Night like sutures seals my eyes;
I am blind as Tiresias,
blinder than a stave.

What is it that makes you save my life?
What insurgence, what obliquity to doubt?
You speak with tall windows,
thatched with roofs—
proofs lie like lilacs
over every stash of slain I bear.

I can hear you in the darkest corner,
acquiescing to the time of day—
and to the day of time—
that in this April can no longer batter me.

I am like a handkerchief pitched, folded,
to the tide of some dark, inward ocean.
Now that sea spins lilac,
salt like mustard seeds
singes to heal.

# Manna

Those who hunger
have no name
for what they hunger for.
Nights, they twist bright cloths
and hold them to their mouths.
Days their hands turn upward,
dry and porous
as split bones.

# After Reading James Kilgo's
## *Deep Enough for Ivorybills*


Like Jim Kilgo,
Augusts, I rode shotgun,
while my mother drove
the battered Chevrolet
across the slate Pee Dee,
toward Pawleys Island and the sea.

I didn't know to look
for Ivorybills.

After Hemingway,
tall trees turned small and twisted.
Window open, I began
to feel the ocean air,
to dream the ocean there;
its rhythms all at once existed
even in the motion of the car.

I leaned out to look;
coastal birds, signals, too,
scrawled white
*v*'s and horizontal slashes.
Gulls, sandpipers, pelicans in flight,
hidden in the sky,
built wings and chests like ivory,
bright sketches,
torn clean and perfect
from seasalt's filigree,
set free to climb and dive.

From the causeway,
houses screened by scattered green
revealed between themselves
solace for all urgency—
sight unlanded sought itself expanded:
blue and lilac, gray and green,
ivory interspersed,
threaded through charged motion.

Augusts, I played patience for return:
*upheavals sprung to rise*
*and fall*
*by ivory-quilled splintered ocean.*

# Departure

Through the red sphere buoy is the Sound:
everything I see turns small.
In the quick of August,
I no longer count:
October air provisions me,
sends covenants unsure.

When we die, I wonder,
will this wind remind us
how earlier we longed
(or crossed ourselves in silence)
as we reached something other,
never, ever wronged.

I will sleep here thirty nights, no more.
When I go, I'll fold the comforter in half,
stack driftwood by the door.
Even if you hear of it
there'll be no elegy, no prayer.

*When she left she was barefoot,*
*there were cyclones in her hair.*

# Peter, the Harp Knight

Early mornings
he runs
down
McKinnon Mountain,
over stones,
into creeks & out again,
until whatever wakes him
stops.

Nobody knows
where he goes;
like afternoon rainstorms
he disappears.

Someone
always fears death,
others claim apparition;
yet every sunrise he's seen,
taking time.

# What For

## after John Berryman

The gentle ambush of your profile
against lifeboats stacked, deflated,
on shelves in emptier rooms,
reminded me of childhood,
with its bright swings and seesaws,
its perilous true mourning.

You were ever lovely and aloof.
May I cross for you glass waters
with both hands tied, eyes impervious, stoically
adrift? May I watch you cross steep streets
to other sides, where armorless you never tried
to gather roses, or the needles of the pine tree,
high, undying?
Nothing in your quiet
or in denying, among rain trees,
offered straws.

Along horizons halt with blue, you moved
to make your studious way.
Against composite walls I stopped to lean,
to stifle words,
what for, I cannot, deftly, say.

## Berryman: Coda

In strife, in plight, in flight,
and in between, he amputated well
wrung limbs, rent torso, but not quite yet
the scrivened mind.
Mind, crazed butcher, hacked him,
harried him to splints.

That was the last sunset throttle,
the last uncluttered, unlit chore.
Into gold clay clouds he trundles,
lone and satcheled evermore.

# After Betrayal

Dear One:
you write
of tables turned over,
wine spilt,
birds loose in empty rooms;
of windows bracketed, doors sealed,
locks unhinged and keyless,
time on your hands.
All along the backyard fence
wisteria curls and spins
its fragrance in air,
no longer August spilt:
wisteria will die
and in its place
vines will blacken, fall.
In the world,
there are not many places
where people know our names.
In the world,
too many highways cross
deep places,
slashed hats and harnesses
beginning to dissolve.

Beds are made to lie in.
Beads are made to string—
or beads are made
to drop behind us
in the trailess wood
where sometimes we must wander,
unacquainted with the animals,
awake or sleeping,
on foot and wandering,
wandering unestranged,
at home.

Sometime
in a September night,
when air calms cooling down,

from the porch
you watch Old Mountain
darken into violet light.
Chimney swifts and wrens embroider
stitches in the sky
and why or what we are
becomes a guess
of less importance than the way
leaves talk back to us
as they settle into rest.

# Walking Pawleys Island

Not for these I raise
The song of thanks and praise;
But for those obstinate questionings
of sense and outward things,
Fallings from us, vanishings . . .
                —Wordsworth, "Intimations of Immortality"

I

Snow this morning patched my jacket
as I tracked the beach,
too bracketed for messages or signs.
Sand dollars tricked to bits, winged
shells in pieces lost to sand—
I walked the sparest splint
of land until it ended.
Accosted by the plight of water giving
over into smoother water,
running out or running in,
I thought to dive.
And then I thought.

Black gulls in flight
dared off the wind;
a yellow leaf descended
out of nowhere down to water,
black. Minutes cracked
and shattered; seconds froze.
I knew at once what someone drowning knows,
those stations of sped life,
where strap by strap
the sting has stunned
and one by one the strings
have sundered until all you hold
is your own stripped other fist.
Fastened so,
there's nowhere else
to go
but down.

## II

On the porch
I let go words' strictures
and look.
This seamless season ties back
its feathers: cold reigns;
down on finite figures
with their crownless hats
the coldness rains.
I walk beaches striped white
to tear new life outward,
arcs arrowed into sea.
Sea's weather rhythms free,
clearly old.
Older, light incarnates,
word of water and bright air,
truest merger of what's pure.
Here, now, for this moment,
heart can sphere this recognition
in its anvil part, the part that breaks
on chords less spare.
In sand, miracles of motion range
downfallen sun; water claims its loss.
On the pier, the "disappointed bridge,"
two fishers cast live strings,
left sunlight glints one instant, breaks.
In my own sewn shoes
I walk tide's wake.
I take the current constancy
for a sign.

## III

The gulls split the creek,
driven inland by the cold. They bank white rigid
wings
against black water.
Afternoon sun behind them lessens;
the golding grip slips low.
Out on the beach
I wear my shadow down,
every human part of me in wraps;
in wraps, too, the inexorable soul
with its wickwings ready, ever,
for a strike.

Water banners, bare light, light
incarnate; I walk light's edge
as it strips the shore of sun.
What happens now can matter
less or more than history has cost;
and if I'm frozen, lost, a shadow
without hands, it matters less,
far less than these blue blades
of ocean that take on light,
bind light into them
like the white gulls' wings
now vanishing through cloud.

IV

> . . . attention . . . , directed toward God, is the very soul
> of prayer.
> —Simone Weil, *Waiting for God*

In rain sometimes
dead missiles surface,
rigless, wires adrift.
(In eyes not here I see
an answer.)
Gulls this morning hinged on rain's hands, swung
or treaded air, denying flight.
I watched the night hush
of a scallop thread gray
and salt's shifts in sand
too fine for prints.

To watch singed-eyed and solemn
as you matter out the afternoon
means more than ignorance
of bloodshame or the wracked ways of stress;
to watch means this: attention—
at tension's curve to balance,
spendthrift and homely,
needier than nails.

If in pieces from sea's deep bracelet
you descry design,
hold still.
Take up that shell and hold it.

In the mortar, in the mine,
confusion may go empty, you may see a sign.

V

> That Christ's incarnation occurred improbably,
> ridiculously, at such and such a time, into such and
> such a place, is referred to . . . as "the scandal of
> particularity."
> —Annie Dillard, *Pilgrim at Tinker Creek*

Even now on the back street
of this ocean town
I can't recall the name
of the baker who ground
his first son to ash flour
and baked him, bread.
I don't remember now exactly how
the blood was traced, or how
he bolted door and window, then replaced
his own insignia with a star.

I can't remember if the wheat
or tares are blessed. It doesn't matter.
Here between sea intersections
I adhere to traffic, lights and lessons,
human motion, gravity's gives and takes.
I watch slow wicks of candles
blue or break. I trick time
by tending miracles, sea wrecks.
Yet in this cautioned stammer
in my sentence against breath
I close consciousness, too, around the one,
the only treachery too true
to be believed.

I listen as I leave the room:
*We need not be deceived.*

# II

Tributes

# Elegy: Michael Egan (1939–1992)

Eight weeks since your good daughter wrote,
six months since cancer turned you under,
over to dark angels and bright stars,
to words' eternity and spheres
of nothingness or light.

Twenty years and more since we tracked
oak shadows down Museum Drive,
leaned back in chairs in Coleman's wake,
while, gentle man and sage, he broke us
into believing in the efficacy
of what others know as grief.
He must have quoted Rilke:
*You must change your life.*

We discovered sacrament in sentences,
rhyme and rhythm, elements of song
and silence, violences of verb.
Each work became a eucharist,
offered and received
beyond the bounds of what we were,
or when we failed, or how
erratically we fought or believed
we believed.

Down by the water at Eddie's Bar,
we pledged unspoken promises,
our trothplight sealed
with alcohol and smoke.
Betrayal, both our frailty,
took you longer.
The last time you telephoned,
I couldn't speak.

And so I mourn you
with my chains drawn tight.
I celebrate your strong beauty
as I celebrate that long legacy,
—words like stars

strung together,
changed, and rearranged
to simplify the darknesses,
the slings and scars,
the solder of each
black and sorrowed night.

# Elegy for a Musician

Already you couldn't play your banjo
when I drove you out from town,
where the carlights burned our eyes
in the winter fog. I shared beer
with you unwisely, I came to know,
for you were restless as I,
and older.

Later when I visited you
in the hospital, I marveled,
fully, at how you balanced
your crutches and your pipe
on the wheelchair's rim
while you blew your harp—

and even later,
when you elevatored up
to roll out and meet me,
chair to chair,
I wondered where
fortitude met dignity,
to edge out your weariness—
I never knew.

Now that your heart's seams
have broken for all time
I learn how deeply far your dreams
go back. I lose track,
remembering.

# Lesson

First day of class
you wrote eleven words
across the board
& wished a poem
from each of us.
*Calliope* & *clown*
were two I knew.
*Barbed wire* made four.

Film ever clouded your gray eyes.
Original Guido, you showed us
light scarecrows dancing in the trees,
ice robins with yellow vests.
You gave us spools
for our bookbags,
spun spells over time.

I still see you
with your comic grin,
extolling heroes.
For you villains were few.

Once you gripped a moth's blue wing,
then let him free.
He ambled upward toward the light,
then ambled down, afraid.

# Another Round

William Harmon, you old scandal,
how do you, with choruses and quints,
survive the doommaster's whip
or the harridan's hoop? How do you
wander over trains' scours
so unscathed and terrorful?

I would invent a verse for you,
arrhythmic and almighty,
if I had a sack of shimmer in my sessions,
a wrest of workingness at all.
Your ruthful voice astounds
as it unharnesses;
it ventures as it strips.
Nothing in the grasp
of that tight festering
involves so plentifully, so tough.

Don't guy now or ever:
I believe in you
as I believe in the raffles
of my mother's mother,
who is nonetheless a saint;
she sifted from this earth
into another ring,
or worthiness of rings.
I still can hear her sing.

# Chatroom

Always
the kitchen table holds
overample conversation,
touchtag feints,
the subtle surplus
of another day.

You lean on the counter
& the circus erupts—
brown bags & silver dishes
clashrattleding.
On the porch computers ping.
The dog turns frantic & when she hears
the bluebird whirr she becomes a blur
of addletry, a sure missile south.
You stuff tomato in your mouth—
no need for more—& prop
your shoulder on the nearest thing.
The phone rings,
you dive, you're all alive,
but nothing's solved, you think,
but the sunlight creases
in newspapers folded
by the stainless sink.

# Moving in Memory

*to Julia Randall*

From Hartley Mill, you name and number proofs:
resiliencies, earth's tenses, celebrations
of earth's sense—bloodroot, jack pine, mayapple,
birch—light tinder for a tracker's fire
against dark traces.

What you never taught me long enough
for sentences to end, I find again
and recognize as real—
Dead Man or Furness Fell,
all conjugations clinch to spell horizons
to the listening eye,
remaker with new alphabets of blues and grays,
reds, lilacs, golds.
No flower holds as long as trees and mountains.
Even transients need rest.

You resolve each wilderness
in increments; syllabic structures
piece the plain flawed swoop of sense.
Over where the light turns dark,
you look for words
to tell us where we are,
or where we were,
maybe in an August night,
with stars like milkweed blowing
down the sky, the moon in its blue satchel,
silver semaphore whose signals try
our torn intentions, our common why.

To till best your own unleavened field,
you work against those obstacles
to fallen nature's weave;
light lifts each metaphor,
swung barriers to grief,
to grave.

# Portrait of Women at Fifty

### I
We begin:
to breathe
like our mothers—

To waver in our worship
of Gramma,
wondering if periods have turned
into ?s, ;s, ,s, :s
—seeing, maybe
only caps (as in capital
& cancer),
space, &, possibly,
the + or the *,
as integral
to our efforts
to commune.

### II
We sign with initials only
because of time or $—
therefore admitting, once
again, how early we were
forced to apprehend
Our Father's middle name
which = Fear.

### III
Laptops hum to us,
when sleep or love abandons,
& we cease to wear aprons,
because now the substances
we spill or waste appear
in flesh & not on
artificial coverings.

Eternally prodigal,
we keep screens clear
although loss or obfuscation
of keys remains a risk.

IV
We read more or less
(sacrificing Russians,
& Catholics, the Orthodox
& the Old).

Similarly, the sacrament
we recognize as True
has more to do
with sex, grandchildren, exercise,
or Art,
than with water, wafer, & Holy Wine—
Hunger &/or Thirst—
or any number
of the 7 Deadlies
which become personified
& shadow us
like prehistorical beasts.

(Obsessions beget obsessions.)

V
If we die
we refuse
interviews.

VI
If we achieve
Fame &/or Riches
(or fail to)—
we deny our fault,
ever pointing
up, down, over,
there,
with hearts covered,
eyes lowered,
moon above unseen,
but recognized,
like an * or star.

# Before Easter

Light breaks down on Tinker Mountain:
Easter Even.
Inside, sun's color catches
in clean wood.

Yesterday, on Tinker Ridge
eight cedar trees
were split by wind;
wood duck near the cove
hid in tunnels where summer beaver bred.
Wind over water resurrected otherworldly shapes
and sky brought down nothing
but another realm of sky.

Through the window we could see
the shed roof peel back,
a silver scab, then fly off
to disappear, like tape.

(Now another day, no longer Friday,
no longer Good, eventide is tempered
by the last light's lace.)

I see a piece of Sunday's *Times*
dissolve in smoke; I know
that when next I sleep to wake
there will be no shadow:
nothing but that dark warmth of this,
born comforter, the light I turn to
when morning moves least far.

## "Motions of the Heart"
### —Pascal


Down the long winds of Route 606,
the dog and I run,
not looking back or down,
moving under sun and into shadow,
out again to where the road wrests
out of sight.

Last night you didn't answer when I called.
I sat outside, on Thomas Arthur's grave
and read inscriptions on neighboring stones.
Graven, words as names arrest the heart
if the heart's at loose, wayfarer restless,
watching for a sign.

We do our best, searching blind:
at night, in other dark, or mindlessly at work
on something rigorous or bare, we do our best.
(Once in a pickup bed, dizzy and too sick
to speak, I understood for seconds how the moon
makes differences in light—nothing little, nothing
new, but something stilling that had to do
with distance and God's air.)

Here on this rock road I can see
no farther than the chestnut branch
just beyond the Thorntons' fence.
I know that, usually, the road keeps on,
that, usually, crossroads happen
and fields fan out east and west
like yesterday's mistakes.
Whatever else I do or do not recognize
as probable or real,
I run.
The dog's ahead of me;
ahead of her, the sun.

# In the Bar

In the bar,
I chew ice
and watch stray straws
from the baskets on the wall
shake and shiver
from the fan's spin.
It's about time
we talked about the shrapnel
and the strong
bridge between us
that breaks and buckles
when you move
too far left;
you go away
too plentifully
and I see shards
of rock and tiny bits
of blood on the sidewalk,
in the street.
The sky slits
and rain resolves
the air
into sheaves of water
that break down
on asphalt, grass
and gravel, on cemetery dirt,
on the steps of enemies
and friends.
A long way from here
a bold man
wakes up shriveled,
and we, who are not to blame,
repeat no vows,
no invocations,
but extend our hands
toward the fan's small wind,
and watch the shadows
shift toward longer
as the sun descends.

# For Now

Darkly, through shrouded shrubbery,
you see your last keeper draw in
his tether, up and leave.
Whether you stave off the gnawed whip
or go along,
botherful and borne,
never matters.

You are he whose half again is halved;
you haven't coast enough to notch the tide.
Walk with your weather cowl outward;
walk with your feather side bound.

# III

Augustine Said

# Good Friday

The impossible fusion impossibly rent,
leveling of inchoate stars;
nature, nothing-knower, slits waterfalls,
smooths hillsides;
the sun shunts off old oceans,
earthover, still.

What does a man do
coming down a ridge
below a hidden town
where cows calm in streets
and chickens sleep?
What does a man do
with his saddlebag or knife,
his yoke so light it loses him?
How does he speak
when night clamps down midafternoon,
when animals and grasses, trees and birds
fold over, sever shadow, disappear?
Does his heart break in an instant,
or does, instantly, his older heart, held closer,
cinch the swerve,
begin to beat?

# Easter

In an empty room like this,
with mountains in the windows
and in the door another door
opening to a corridor,
with light in crosses,
light like current
up and down the bridled air.

In an empty room like this,
what does it mean
that when I take the page
and turn it,
songs thread up through air,
and, in between,
a quiet,
like a strong hand,
weaves
the parcels,
ties the parcels over
onto one another's backs?

This is morning.
There are clean shelves,
and sun sweeps the room and sweeps it again.
*I can spell mercy*
*in fourteen languages:*
*chesid misericordia chesid grace:*
*I can spell mercy.*

And vases tip over,
water spills like light
(daisies, daffodils,
the lily and the pearl).

It is Easter,
every second,
in an empty room like this,
with the last song
ending
as another begins.

# Farmer

You plant white pines
while the sun collapses:
Easter Even,
your child beside you
hefts a rock
three times his weight
and lets it fall.
Earth, not air, not water,
not fire, is elemental
to you now, without your shirt,
the sweat-cool stripes
against the skin
that holds you in.
It gives to you a shadow
that light defines
less and less,
as it falls down
among loblolly, sycamore,
birch trees with stalks
so white
that even when this night
at last consents
to lean against the ground
they branch up sudden,
trim stalks so bright
they seem
like holy straws
a farmer can grip—
when history and husbandry
erect stiff boundaries
to vision,
to singling out
the best
that he has sown.

## If Love Is a Forest

Augustine said
that everything we do
is dangerous.
I believe him.

Lists of verbs
collaborate to ambush,
collaborate to drive us
through the outskirts
into mecklenburgs of woe.

This is the day
when the sun wants
nothing more
than to spill its light
against the notchedness of crime,
when light like insurrection
tears the world apart
and lifts
into a larger, spendthrift space.

If love is a forest,
then anyone can
make a friend of trees,
those tall, tough temples
where to worship means
(first of all)—
to cross your heart,
and have to die
for leaves and sepals,
for air among them
that rains upward
to let them fly.

# Dame Julian of Norwich

### I
Dear Anna:

Breath here is simpler.
Anemones and violets break open
into light, long-shingled, steady.
On rain trees, leaves of water
interlace and shimmer
when sun splits shadow,
afternoons.

In the woods,
blue boys lift rifles,
slick with oil,
and till hulled light
from blackened branches.

*Jesus is our own true mother,*
Dame Julian of Norwich writes.

Hierarchies here enforce each pattern.
Earth in its blue sling abolishes no tie.
More orderly than rain or fire, we work.
We verify the sky.

### II
I believe the lessons of the interstate
go lost tonight, the low moon
like a ladle, measuring spilled sky.
Still, why we look to carriages, to spurs,
I don't know.
Cars spool by: raindrops on knife blades,
they disappear, or show up afterward,
disguised as hand prints, hoofprints, harps.

You wonder, as you stare off,
whose horizons suddenly grow dim
or, jagged-edged, slow splendidly
to dust. They disappear.

You wonder as you watch.
Dame Julian recognized lost as *sanctus;*
strait highway; *mother;* finally,
the moon's most tilled, most sacrificial fire.

### III
I write to you of blue boys
in woods holding guns,
of light on gunbarrels,
long glints like rods.
I write of Julian of Norwich
and Christ *our own true mother,*
Dame Julian the anchoress,
whose hidden blood
drew supernatural light from air,
who prayed for wounds
to heal her.
Wounded, she knew at last
the cross was love:
*Christ lives in me.*

The boys no longer
shoot at deer along Bear Creek.
Quail listen in fallen light,
and nighttime herds hear children,
running home.

To Julian,
Christ our mother came
to spring her from her cell.
He let her know,
and not too early,
*I shall make all things well.*

# Merton

... That you may become the brother of
God and learn to know the Christ of the
burnt men.

—Thomas Merton, *The Seven-
Storey Mountain*

How, when your eyes try long enough
God's traces in the fusion
of all forces and all fire,
how, then, can you come to bear desire,
and know quick dust,
among the candles,
with its own deft patterns
no one sees or simplifies the same?

There is no question.
The Christ of the burnt men
shook you free—
free of hatchet tolls and lightning quills,
of the human schism.
Solitary in the wind
you came to know, unsigned,
the Mother's slain embrace,
while in pieces all around you
mansions, multitudes, merde, mirth
receded, every checkered votary or plain:

*a man alone, Christ-burnt and storied,
singlehearted in the light's one strain.*

# Prayer for the Whole State

### All Saints' Day

Under cover, volcanic and alone,
you rivet rage to sun straps
as they bind the room.
It is never earlier, never later
than the heart's bell sprung,
wrung.

Grievous everywhere, small people rant and hide.
The world's acrostics break.
Each of several continents divides.
Women lead babies, hungry, eyes wide;
fathers vie and vie and vie
into night perpetual
until little people die:
they don't get up.

Stiff strife in cleated shoes
stalks mightier and full.
Any hour and all at once
merriment and murder sear, astound.
Famine blasts. Fire and ornament expound.

And somewhere, in the distance,
all around a yew tree,
servants gather on their knees.
The bartered tree lights higher.
There are meadows in the breeze.

# For All the Saints

### I

Saint Michael and all angels, raft us.
Over timber, over void, over all unravelings,
all loss, stick near us and prevail.
The sick will tatters, like a scarf,
it rattles in the wind.
My friend, my brother's battered eyes discover
ruined chimneys, waste.
Stories of the sun enchant us and we sleep,
or down in unmade graves we cower,
without dance; we weep.

### II

Gabriel, or Raphael, you play for us
such harmonies of halves and wholes
the deepest wells within us brim.
This is the hour of sickles pocketed,
blades pulled down.
My friend, my brother angel whirls a crown
into wide air that whirrs to stars
that will not fall.
Whatever in this morning you foretell,
we will not strip the rosary
nor abdicate the bell.

# IV

Rivets

*New Poems*

# Early Morning, Winter

### I

Saint Lucy's day approaches
& the moon through water
swims upward to disappear.

Far upward,
we wander,
on a lake,
far over
where now mallards rest
featherless heads
under wings.
(Poor things.)

### II

Bakers fling light crusts
to a waitless brood.
(All food is good
this morning
as the lark sings
so early
none can rise.)

Too soon:
our occasion is over.

### III

Remember Juan Dunbar—
his small suit of white—
he ran after dusk
to the Muse's blue hill;
the ducks on that point
still take notice.

Who will he sing to now?
Who will arise to tell
how grackles hold gold
so close to their chests
no blackbird's vest
can prove blue?

# Trainsong

They say: follow them,
follow them until they crash,
or collide, or intersect, and become *one*!

There are many trains immaterial to most.
The loco-motive, snakeblinder, from ghostly towns,
downs into suntracks in caverns, burns horizons,
and backs again to meet its mate, the wagontrain.
Wagontrains, ever for the birds, carry:
iron, coal, big folks and little folks,
animals, daisies, crates,
windowsills and windshields,
corn for fields, beans, bait, fish,
fowl—they carry almost any-
*thing*, even *paleontol*, computers!

Once on a train to Lake Charles, Louisiana,
I drank beer and ate shellfish in the barcar
with two strangers. They made me laugh until I cried,
then we ate fried froglegs and green tomatoes,
summer upon us, cotton and sweet corn in the fields.

# Weatherman

*to LDR*

### I

From the fire tower
eight counties are visible.
Watchmen take turns
and if a tree burns
no one reports it.
"Natural," they claim.

The names of the counties
matter little. But each lies
endangered in racks of heat and cold,
hailstorm or lightning, waterfall or creeks,
ice & avalanching snow.

### II

The meteorologist visits
daily with his furrowed brow
and tripod scope.
He can see for hours,
for half-lives of star dust,
and half-lives of clay.
Days of fine rain
find him most awake
in his cleated boots
with his red socks
folded just so.

He can recite the names
of every rock, blade, or stem.
He has learned, in silence,
gatherings of planets, of stars.
Men think he is mighty;
they look to him for news.

# Kalanchoe

Reclining out from town
on Clem Roberts' farm,
like bits of sockeye salmon,
or flags torn by wind,
you hold back, this spring,
your opulent flowers—
a stuttered armada
at risk for a sign.

No bells trill—
from here to Yanceyville
nothing but pools pearl
the dirt & red clay
like wounds runs
into green; machines,
faltered in sheds
at this hour,
not only disappear,
but offer no shadow,
*no red rock,*
behind which to hide.

No one's brother rides
ranges here; no one's
pet tiger slips behind a cypress knee,
eyes like gold flame.

*My name is legion.*

Mother of thousands—
they claim—
and what is that to us?

*Our* name is legion
and, oh, the wheat speaks—

tonight the weather
turns its back on you—
ice crops up

in January places—
March a notecard
underfoot.

But you live
as we do.
Your stern black
sockets
hold everything
you need.

# Still Life

Monday afternoon
in the village,
stenciled glass chimes
crash in October rain.

January snowfall,
twenty fingers deep,
still sleeps, like a chrysalis
under green.

# Sower of Light

Bridges collapse
once we're across—
loose scalework
and rafter
like steep satin sheen—
But, Lord God,
when birds surface
from water or dust,
there's night gone to pieces,
no minion to trust—

we sing of Christ's sorrow—
his bondage, his wear—
we sing terror bodied
in thorntemplate hair

*Black Lady, forgive us*
*our fortunate strain:*
*our bodies so tortured,*
*our minds so awry,*
*forgive us*
*the needle,*
*the staggered, blank eye—*

# Jets

Tell me about jet rags.
Tell me about the vertical daggers
in the road all pointing north.
Tell me about Moon Pies & Cokes
you buy conveniently as you drive,
jokes men toss at you
through windows like soiled socks.

Say you are twenty:
you leave the house alone at dusk,
crank up the engine to sail sunset back
to *your* state now, Virginia, New York,
or Maryland—it makes all of the difference.
When you hit the road to Gretna
you change your mind:
you flip the switch,
cut cruise control, decide:
you'll stay at the Greenwood,
Route 315, have some fried chicken,
some turnip greens and a cup or two of joe,
one to go so that you can slip into the night
& walk that deep hill to the place where the counties
split and the country roils and rambles
like a feverish dream.

That coffee will slosh
but that's fine: all will be well,
*all manner of thing shall be well*
and you'll wake earlier than the sun
and run down Route 315 as far as you can,
until you see a farmer pitching hay—
there will be new calves in the meadow,
corn in the crib.

You'll know, somehow,
you'll run that route
as long as it takes
to make the byways safe
for every mad dog, every hen.

# Report on "A"

Still, she believes light
an animate creature—
one to gambol with—
to dance about & kiss.

It's in her blood,
this obsession
to play with what
is most dangerous
& fair.

She races through
ashes of the manger
to spangle-shattered trees—
she's nobody's.
She exceeds all boundaries
for the sheer plain swerve—
vertical, white.

When we look for her,
she's gone.

# Beetles

Shall we go out now
     after the rain
& buy Beetles?
*Red ones, snow ones, green ones,*
Blue. Or shall we hop, skip, & sprint
to the nearest pharmacy & buy some meds?
Or a pup—a pug or a chow—some-
thang to watch over now that the trucks
have left & red clay covers all roads?

It is too fretful to decide how to spend.
Especially when all checks bend
both ways & the longer the day is
the less the cash.

We might sail, instead, to Byzantium,
catch some rays. Catch some rays
& fill our ways with treasures,
immaterial & vast. I am but a beggar
on a lowly street, rained on & frightful.
If a Beetle pass this way, shall I wave
& be brave or crudely kick some mud?
Yeats might call a tossup; more likely,
he'd hitch a ride. Beetles look so spanking,
especially after rain.